Southern Cor

Sides, Main Dishes & More!

S. L. Watson

Copyright © 2017 S. L. Watson

All rights reserved.

ISBN: 9781731587565

All rights reserved. No part of this book may be reproduced or utilized in any form or by any means, electronic or mechanical, including photocopying and recording without express written permission from the author and/or copyright holder.

This book is for informational or entertainment purposes only. Cover design S. L. Watson 2018. Picture courtesy of Canva.

The author has made every effort to ensure the information provided in this book is correct. Failure to follow directions could result in a failed recipe. The author does not assume and hereby disclaim any liability to any party for any loss, damage, illness or disruption caused by errors and omissions, whether such errors and omissions result from negligence, accident or any other cause.

The author has made every effort to provide accurate information in the creation of this book. The author accepts no responsibility and gives no warranty for any damages or loss of any kind that might be incurred by the reader or user due to actions resulting from the use of the information in this book. The user assumes complete responsibility for the use of the information in this book.

DEDICATION

To corn lover's everywhere!

CONTENTS

	Introduction	i
1	Appetizers & Dips	1
2	Main Dishes & Casseroles	10
3	Breads	23
4	Soups, Salads & Sides	34

INTRODUCTION

Corn is great anytime of the year. When the fresh corn is ready in the garden, I am always looking for ways to use corn. Canned or frozen corn is a great substitute for fresh corn in the recipes. Corn is versatile and can be added to most main dishes. Whether you use corn as a side dish or add corn to stretch a main meal, it is a tasty way to eat vegetables.

With 100 recipes, you are sure to find a new family favorite. Included are recipes for corn on the cob, appetizers, soups, side dishes, breads and main dishes. Corn make soups hearty and filling. Sample recipes include Grilled Corn Salsa, Beefy Corn Nachos, Black Bean & Corn Pork Chops, Smoky Corn and Chicken Salad, Cheesy Corn Pie, Grilled Corn with Maple Vinaigrette, Creole Cornbread and Cajun Corn Chowder.

1 APPETIZERS & DIPS

Corn makes appetizers more filling. The added flavor and fiber are also a bonus.

Hot Corn Dip

Makes 3 cups

2 cups cooked whole kernel corn
8 oz. can diced green chiles, drained
1/2 cup chopped red bell pepper
1 cup shredded Monterey Jack cheese
2 tbs. chopped and seeded jalapeno pepper
1 cup mayonnaise
1/2 cup grated Parmesan cheese
2 tbs. sliced black olives
Tortilla chips

This dip will not work with light or low fat mayonnaise. In a mixing bowl, add the corn, green chiles, red bell pepper, Monterey Jack cheese, jalapeno pepper, mayonnaise and Parmesan cheese. Stir until well combined. Spoon the dip into a 2 quart casserole dish.

Preheat the oven to 350°. Bake for 30 minutes or until the dip is hot and bubbly. Remove the dip from the oven and sprinkle the black olives over the dip. Serve hot with tortilla chips.

Field Pea & Corn Dip

Makes 8 cups

This is so good with corn chips, crispy cornbread or served as a side dish.

2 cans drained field peas with snaps, 15 oz. size
3 cups cooked whole kernel corn
2 cans diced tomatoes with green chiles, 10 oz. size
14 oz. can diced tomatoes with juice
5 diced green onions
16 oz. bottle Italian dressing
2 garlic cloves, minced
1 tbs. finely chopped fresh parsley

Add all the ingredients to a large bowl. Stir until all the ingredients are combined. Cover the bowl and chill for 8 hours. Drain off the liquid before serving.

Mexicorn Salsa

Makes 3 cups

2 1/2 cups whole kernel corn, cooked
1 tomato, diced
1 jalapeno pepper, seeded and minced
1 garlic clove, minced
4 oz. can green chiles with juice
1/4 cup sliced green onions
2 tbs. olive oil
2 tbs. white vinegar
1/2 tsp. salt

Add all the ingredients to a serving bowl. Toss until combined. Cover the bowl and chill for 3 hours before serving. Serve on chips, toasted baguette slices, pork or chicken.

Corn and Avocado Salsa

Makes 4 1/2 cups

4 cups fresh or frozen whole kernel corn
1 tbs. fajita seasoning
1/2 tsp. black pepper
2 tbs. vegetable oil
1 red bell pepper, chopped
2 tbs. chopped jalapeno pepper
1/2 cup chopped green onion
1/4 cup chopped fresh cilantro
1/4 cup fresh lime juice
2 tbs. orange juice
3/4 tsp. salt
2 ripe avocados, peeled, pitted and diced

In a large skillet over medium heat, add the corn, fajita seasoning, black pepper and vegetable oil. Saute the corn for 8 minutes or until the corn is lightly browned. Remove the skillet from the heat. Cool the corn for 20 minutes.

Add the corn, red bell pepper, jalapeno pepper, green onion, cilantro, lime juice, orange juice, salt and avocados to a serving bowl. Toss until all the ingredients are combined. Cover the bowl and chill for 30 minutes before serving.

Grilled Corn Salsa

Serve this salsa with chips, beef, pork or poultry.

Makes 5 cups

3 ears fresh corn, grilled
1 large purple onion, cut into 1/2" slices and grilled
1 red bell pepper, halved and grilled
2 large tomatoes, seeded and chopped
2 jalapeno peppers, seeded and minced
2 garlic cloves, minced
1/4 cup chopped fresh cilantro
1/2 tsp. salt
1/4 tsp. ground cumin
1 tbs. olive oil
1 tbs. lime juice

Remove the corn from the cob. Add all the ingredients to a large bowl. Toss until combined. Cover the bowl and chill the salsa at least 2 hours before serving. The salsa taste best if left to chill for 12 hours before serving.

Roasted Corn & Avocado Dip

Makes 3 cups

1 cup frozen whole kernel corn, thawed
2 tsp. vegetable oil
2 avocados, peeled
1 tomato, finely chopped
3 tbs. fresh lime juice
2 tbs. minced onion
2 garlic cloves, minced
1 tbs. jalapeno pepper, minced
1/2 tsp. salt
1/4 tsp. ground cumin

Preheat the oven to 400°. Place the corn and vegetable oil in a shallow baking dish. Stir until combined. Bake for 8 minutes or until the corn is lightly browned. Stir the corn every 3 minutes. Remove the corn from the oven and cool completely.

Mash 1 avocado and chop the other avocado. Place the avocados in a serving bowl. Add the corn, tomato, lime juice, onion, garlic, jalapeno pepper, salt and cumin. Toss until combined. Cover the bowl and refrigerate until chilled. Serve with corn chips or tortilla chips.

Chorizo Corn Relish

Makes 2 cups

2 large ears fresh corn
1/2 cup chorizo sausage
1/2 cup diced red bell pepper
1/2 cup diced green bell pepper
2 green onions, chopped
1 ancho chile, seeded and chopped
1/2 cup chopped fresh cilantro
1 1/2 tbs. fresh lime juice
1 tbs. maple syrup

Remove the corn from the cob. In a skillet over medium high heat, add the corn and chorizo sausage. Stir constantly to keep the corn and chorizo from burning. Cook for several minutes or until the sausage is well browned and the corn is tender.

Add the red bell pepper, green bell pepper, green onions, ancho chile, cilantro, lime juice and maple syrup. Stir constantly and cook for 3 minutes. Remove the skillet from the heat and serve.

Serve the relish over meats or with crackers.

Corn Relish

Makes 4 cups

2 cans drained whole kernel corn, 16 oz. size
4 oz. jar diced red pimentos, drained
1/2 cup red bell pepper, chopped
2 tbs. vegetable oil
1/2 cup granulated sugar
1/2 cup vinegar
2 tsp. dried minced onion
1/4 tsp. celery seeds
1/8 tsp. salt

In a heat proof mixing bowl, add the corn, red pimentos, red bell pepper and vegetable oil. Toss until well combined. In a small sauce pan over medium heat, add the granulated sugar, vinegar, onion, celery seeds and salt. Bring the sauce to a boil. When the sauce is boiling, reduce the heat to low.

Place a lid on the pan and simmer the sauce for 2 minutes. Remove the pan from the heat and pour the sauce over the vegetables in the bowl. Toss until well combined. Cover the bowl and chill the relish for 2 hours before serving.

Serve the relish over beans, meats, vegetables or use in salads.

Sweet Corn and Tomato Relish

Serve this relish over crab cakes, fish or beans.

Makes 3 cups

2 cups sweet white corn, cooked
2 large tomatoes, peeled and chopped
3 green onions, sliced
2 tbs. lemon juice
1 tbs. olive oil
1/2 tsp. salt
1/2 tsp. black pepper
1/4 tsp. garlic salt
1/8 tsp. Tabasco sauce

Add all the ingredients to a mixing bowl. Toss until well combined. Cover the bowl and chill the relish for 3 hours before serving.

2 MAIN DISHES & CASSEROLES

Corn is mainly used as a side dish but use corn to elevate a main dish. Corn is a great way to add nutrition to your main dish. It stretches the dish and is a great way to use an inexpensive vegetable.

Beefy Corn Nachos

Makes 6 servings

1 lb. ground beef
2 cups cooked whole kernel corn
1/4 cup diced green bell pepper
1/4 cup diced red bell pepper
14 oz. can diced tomatoes with juice
2 tbs. taco seasoning mix
8 oz. Mexican Velveeta cheese, cubed
6 oz. bag nacho cheese chips

In a large skillet over medium heat, add the ground beef. Stir frequently to break the ground beef into crumbles. Cook about 6 minutes or until the ground beef is well browned and no longer pink. Drain off the excess grease.

Add the corn, green bell pepper, red bell pepper, tomatoes, taco seasoning mix and Velveeta cheese to the skillet. Stir constantly and cook until the cheese melts. Remove the skillet from the heat.

Place the nacho cheese chips on a large serving platter. Spoon the ground beef topping over the chips and serve.

Hamburger Corn Casserole

Makes 8 servings

1 1/2 lbs. ground beef
1 1/4 cups chopped onion
6 oz. medium egg noodles, cooked
10.75 oz. can cream of chicken soup
10.75 oz. can cream of mushroom soup
2 cups cooked whole kernel corn
2 oz. jar diced red pimentos, drained
1 cup sour cream
1 cup fine dry breadcrumbs
2 tbs. unsalted butter, cut into small pieces

In a large skillet over medium heat, add the ground beef and onion. Stir frequently to break the ground beef into crumbles as it cooks. Cook about 7 minutes or until the ground beef is well browned and no longer pink. Drain all the grease from the ground beef.

Add the noodles, cream of chicken soup, cream of mushroom soup, corn, red pimentos and sour cream to the skillet. Stir until combined and cook only until all the ingredients are thoroughly heated. Remove the skillet from the heat.

Preheat the oven to 350°. Spray a 9 x 13 casserole dish with non stick cooking spray. Spoon the skillet contents into the casserole dish. Sprinkle the breadcrumbs over the top of the casserole. Place the butter pieces over the breadcrumbs. Bake for 45 minutes or until the casserole is bubbly and the breadcrumbs golden brown. Remove the casserole from the oven and serve.

Corn Stuffed Butterfly Pork Chops

Makes 4 servings

1 1/2 cups frozen whole kernel corn, thawed
1 1/2 cups soft breadcrumbs
1 tbs. minced fresh parsley
1 tbs. finely chopped onion
3/4 tsp. rubbed sage
3/4 tsp. salt
1/4 tsp. black pepper
1 egg
3 tbs. whole milk
4 bone in pork chops, 1 1/2" thick
2 tbs. vegetable oil
1/4 cup water

In a mixing bowl, add the corn, breadcrumbs, parsley, onion, sage, salt and black pepper. Stir until all the ingredients are combined. In a shallow bowl, add the egg and milk. Whisk until well combined and add to the corn mixture. Toss until all the ingredients are combined.

Cut a pocket on the meaty side of each pork chop. Cut the pocket almost all the way to the bone. Stuff each pocket with 1/4 cup corn mixture. Secure the pocket closed with toothpicks if needed.

In a skillet over medium heat, add the vegetable oil. When the oil is hot, add the pork chops. Brown the pork chops for 3 minutes on each side. Remove the skillet from the heat.

Preheat the oven to 350°. Spray a 9 x 13 casserole dish with non stick cooking spray. Place the pork chops in the casserole dish. Pour the water around the pork chops. Cover the dish with a lid or aluminum foil. Bake for 1 hour or until the pork chops are no longer pink and tender. Remove the pork chops from the oven and cool for 5 minutes before serving.

Baked Black Bean & Corn Salsa Pork Chops

Makes 4 servings

1 oven cooking bag
1 tbs. all purpose flour
1/2 tsp. garlic powder
1/2 tsp. salt
1/2 tsp. black pepper
2 1/2 cups cooked whole kernel corn
15 oz. can black beans, drained and rinsed
10 oz. can diced tomatoes with green chiles
4 boneless pork chops, 1/2" thick

Preheat the oven to 350°. Add the all purpose flour, 1/4 teaspoon garlic powder, 1/4 teaspoon salt and 1/4 teaspoon black pepper to the oven bag. Twist the end of the bag and shake until all the ingredients are combined.

Add the whole kernel corn, black beans and diced tomatoes with juice to the bag. Twist the bag and shake until the vegetables are combined. Sprinkle 1/4 teaspoon garlic powder, 1/4 teaspoon salt and 1/4 teaspoon black pepper over the pork chops. Place the pork chops over the vegetables in the bag. Close the bag with the tie included with the bag. Place the bag on a baking sheet. With a sharp knife, cut six slits in the bag to allow the steam to escape.

Bake for 30 minutes or until the pork chops are no longer pink and tender. Remove the pork chops from the oven and cool for 5 minutes before opening the bag.

Grilled Mexican Pork Chops

Makes 4 servings

4 boneless pork chops, 1/2" thick
1/2 tsp. salt
1 tsp. chili powder
30 oz. jar chunky salsa
15 oz. can kidney beans, rinsed and drained
1 1/2 cups fresh or frozen whole kernel corn
1/2 cup dry long grain rice
1 cup shredded Mexican cheese blend

Place four sheets heavy duty aluminum foil on your work surface. Place one pork chop in the center of each piece of aluminum foil. Sprinkle the salt and chili powder over the pork chops. Spoon the salsa, kidney beans, corn and rice over the pork chops.

Fold each aluminum foil sheet into a packet. Have your grill hot and ready. Place the packets on the grill. Cook for 40 minutes or until the pork chops are no longer pink and tender. The corn should be tender when ready. Remove the packets from the grill.

Cool the pork chops for 5 minutes before opening the packets. Carefully open the packets and sprinkle the Mexican cheese blend over the top of the pork chops before serving.

Smoky Corn & Chicken Salad

Makes 4 servings

3/4 cup ranch dressing
2 chipotle peppers in adobo sauce
1 tbs. unsalted butter
2 cups frozen whole kernel corn, thawed
8 cups romaine lettuce, torn into bite size pieces
3 cups shredded cooked chicken
1 1/2 cups chopped tomato
1/3 cup diced purple onion
1 cup croutons

In a small bowl, add the ranch dressing and chipotle peppers. Stir until combined. In a skillet over medium heat, add the butter. When the butter melts, add the corn. Saute the corn for 6 minutes or until the corn is tender. Remove the skillet from the heat.

In a serving bowl, add the lettuce, chicken, tomato, onion and corn. Toss until the salad is combined. Drizzle the ranch dressing over the salad. Toss until combined. Sprinkle the croutons over the top and serve.

Sauteed Spicy Sausage & Corn Salad

Makes 4 servings

8 oz. spicy smoked sausage, diced
1/2 cup chopped onion
1/2 cup chopped green bell pepper
2 garlic cloves, minced
3 cups fresh corn kernels
1 cup sliced fresh okra
1 cup peeled and diced tomato
Salt and black pepper to taste

In a large skillet over medium heat, add the smoked sausage. Saute the sausage for 4 minutes or until the sausage is well browned. Add the onion, green bell pepper and garlic to the skillet. Saute the vegetables for 5 minutes. Add the corn, okra and tomato to the skillet. Saute the vegetables for 10 minutes or until the corn is tender. Remove the skillet from the heat and season to taste with salt and black pepper before serving.

Andouille & Corn Skillet

Makes 6 servings

2 cups chopped onion
1/2 cup chopped green bell pepper
3 tbs. olive oil
6 cups fresh whole kernel corn
2 fresh tomatoes, diced
3/4 lb. cooked andouille sausage, diced
1/2 cup chopped green onion tops
1/2 tsp. salt
1/4 tsp. black pepper

In a large skillet over medium heat, add the onion, green bell pepper and olive oil. Saute the onion and green bell pepper for 10 minutes. Add the corn, tomatoes and andouille sausage to the skillet.

Stir frequently and cook for 15 minutes. The corn should be tender when ready. Remove the skillet from the heat. Add the green onion tops, salt and black pepper to the skillet. Stir until combined and serve.

Simple Chicken Corn Wraps

Makes 4 servings

2 cups cubed cooked chicken
2 cups cooked whole kernel corn
1 cup salsa
1 cup shredded cheddar cheese
4 warmed flour tortillas, 6" size

Spoon the chicken and corn down the center of each tortilla. Spoon the salsa over the filling. Sprinkle the cheddar cheese over the filling. Wrap the tortillas up and serve.

Grilled Corn & Squash Quesadillas

Makes 6 servings

4 ears fresh corn, husk removed
4 yellow squash, halved lengthwise
1 cup thinly sliced onion
2 jalapeno peppers
2 tbs. minced fresh basil
3 tsp. minced fresh oregano
2 garlic cloves, minced
1/2 tsp. salt
1/2 tsp. ground cumin
12 flour tortillas, 8" size
2 cups shredded Monterey Jack cheese
2 tbs. vegetable oil

Have your grill hot and ready. Place the corn, squash, sliced onion and jalapeno peppers on the grill. Turn frequently and cook for 10 minutes or until the vegetables are tender. Remove the vegetables from the grill and cool for 10 minutes.

Remove the corn from the cob and place in a large bowl. Chop the squash and add to the bowl. Seed and dice the jalapeno peppers. Add the jalapeno peppers and sliced onions to the bowl. Add the basil, oregano, garlic, salt and cumin to the bowl. Stir until all the ingredients are combined.

Place 1/2 cup corn filling on one side of each tortilla. Sprinkle the Monterey Jack cheese over the filling. Fold the tortilla over the filling. In a large skillet over medium heat, add 1 tablespoon vegetable oil. When the oil is hot, add half the tortillas. Cook for 2 minutes on each side or until the tortillas begin to brown. Remove the tortillas from the skillet. Repeat the step cooking the remaining tortillas. Serve the quesadillas hot.

Cheesy Corn Pie

Makes a 10" pie

2 cups Bisquick
2 tbs. melted unsalted butter
1/2 cup cold water
1/2 cup whole milk
4 eggs
16 oz. can cream style corn
3/4 cup shredded sharp cheddar cheese
2 tbs. minced onion
2 tbs. minced green bell pepper
1/4 tsp. black pepper

In a mixing bowl, add the Bisquick, butter and cold water. Stir until well combined and the batter is stiff. Spray a 10" pie pan with non stick cooking spray. Spoon the batter into the pie pan. The batter will be your crust so spoon the batter up the sides of the pan.

Preheat the oven to 375°. In a mixing bowl, add the milk and eggs. Whisk until well combined. Add the corn, cheddar cheese, onion, green bell pepper and black pepper. Whisk until well combined and pour the filling into the pie pan. Bake for 50 minutes or until the pie is set. A knife inserted in the center of the pie will come out clean when ready.

Corn and Squash Frittata

Makes 4 servings

1 cup fresh corn, cut from the cob
2 eggs, beaten
2 tbs. all purpose flour
1/4 tsp. baking powder
1/4 tsp. salt
1/4 tsp. black pepper
1 zucchini, unpeeled and grated
1 1/2 tbs. unsalted butter

Scrape the cob to remove as much of the milk as possible from the cob. Add the corn and any milk from the cob to a mixing bowl. Add the eggs, all purpose flour, baking powder, salt, black pepper and zucchini to the bowl. Whisk until well combined.

In an 8" non stick skillet, add the butter. When the butter melts, pour half the butter into the egg mixture. Whisk until combined. Pour the egg mixture over the remaining butter in the skillet. Reduce the heat to low and place a lid on the skillet. Cook about 15 minutes or until the frittata is set. Remove the frittata from the heat and serve.

Country Corn Omelet

Makes 6 servings

4 strips bacon
4 tbs. unsalted butter
1 onion, chopped
1 cup cooked whole kernel corn
4 cups shredded kale or collard greens
8 eggs
1/2 cup shredded Monterey Jack cheese
1/3 cup sour cream

In a skillet over medium heat, add the bacon. Cook the bacon for 6-7 minutes or until the bacon is crisp. Remove the bacon from the skillet and drain on paper towels. Crumble the bacon into pieces. Leave the bacon drippings in the skillet.

Add the onion and 2 tablespoons butter to the skillet. Saute the onion for 4-5 minutes or until the onion is tender. Add the corn and kale to the skillet. Saute the vegetables for 4 minutes. Remove the skillet from the heat.

In a separate skillet, add 2 tablespoons butter over medium low heat. In a mixing bowl, add the eggs. Whisk the eggs until well combined. When the butter melts, add the eggs. As the eggs begin to set, push the edges of the eggs under so the uncooked eggs will flow underneath. Keep pushing the eggs until set. This will take about 4-5 minutes. When the eggs are set but still creamy, spoon the vegetables over one side of the eggs. Sprinkle the cheese over the vegetables. Spoon the sour cream in the center of the vegetables.

Flip the other side of the omelet over the filling and serve.

3 BREADS

Cornbread is the most popular use for corn in breads. Included are a few of my favorite cornbreads featuring corn as an extra addition.

Cheddar Cornbread

Makes 12 servings

3 tbs. vegetable oil
2 pkgs. cornbread muffin mix, 8 oz. size
2 beaten eggs
1/2 cup whole milk
1/2 cup plain yogurt
15 oz. can cream style corn
1/2 cup shredded cheddar cheese

Preheat the oven to 400°. Do not use a glass baking pan for this recipe. The difference in temperatures may cause the glass to break. In a 9 x 13 baking pan, add the vegetable oil. Place the oil in the oven and heat until the pan and oil are sizzling hot.

In a mixing bowl, add the cornbread muffin mix, eggs, milk, yogurt, corn and cheddar cheese. Stir until combined. Pour the batter into the hot pan. Bake for 20 minutes or until a toothpick inserted in the center of the cornbread comes out clean. Remove the pan from the oven and serve.

Crawfish Cornbread

Makes a 9 x 13 baking pan

1 cup finely chopped onion
1/2 cup finely chopped green bell pepper
1/2 cup plus 2 tbs. vegetable oil
2 jalapeno peppers, seeded and minced
2 cups plain white or yellow cornmeal
3 tsp. baking powder
1 tsp. salt
1/2 tsp. baking soda
3 eggs
1 cup whole milk
15 oz. can cream style corn
1 1/2 cups shredded cheddar cheese
3/4 cup sliced green onion
1 cup cooked crawfish meat

Preheat the oven to 400°. Add 2 tablespoons vegetable oil to a 9 x 13 baking pan. Place the pan in the oven and cook until the pan and oil are sizzling hot.

In a skillet over medium heat, add 1 tablespoon vegetable oil. When the oil is hot, add the onion and green bell pepper. Saute the onion and green bell pepper for 5 minutes. Remove the skillet from the heat and stir in the jalapeno peppers.

In a mixing bowl, add the cornmeal, baking powder, salt and baking soda. Whisk until all the dry ingredients are combined. Add the vegetables from the skillet, the remaining vegetable oil, eggs, milk, corn, cheddar cheese, green onion and crawfish. Stir only until the batter is moistened and combined.

Spoon the batter into the hot pan. Bake for 40 minutes or until a toothpick inserted in the center of the cornbread comes out clean and the cornbread is golden brown. Remove the pan from the oven and serve.

Creole Cornbread

Makes a 10" cast iron skillet

2 cups cooked rice
1 cup plain yellow cornmeal
1/2 cup chopped onion
2 tbs. chopped jalapeno pepper
1 tsp. salt
1/2 tsp. baking soda
2 eggs
1 cup whole milk
1/4 cup plus 2 tbs. vegetable oil
2 cups cream style corn
3 cups shredded cheddar cheese

Preheat the oven to 350°. In a mixing bowl, add the rice, cornmeal, onion, jalapeno pepper, salt and baking soda. Stir until combined. In a separate bowl, add the eggs, milk, 1/4 cup vegetable oil, corn and cheddar cheese. Whisk until well combined and add to the dry ingredients. Stir until well combined.

Place 2 tablespoons vegetable oil in a 10" cast iron skillet. Place the skillet in the oven until the skillet and oil are sizzling hot. Pour the batter into the hot skillet. Bake for 45 minutes or until the center of the cornbread is done and golden brown. Remove the skillet from the oven and serve.

Whole Kernel Corn Cornbread

Makes a 10" cast iron skillet

2 tbs. vegetable oil
1 cup fresh or frozen whole kernel corn
1 cup whole milk
1/4 cup honey
2 tbs. melted unsalted butter
2 eggs
3/4 cup all purpose flour
1/4 cup oat bran flour
1 cup plain white or yellow cornmeal
4 tsp. baking powder
3/4 tsp. salt

Preheat the oven to 400°. Add the vegetable oil to a 10" cast iron skillet. Place the skillet in the oven and heat until the oil and skillet are sizzling hot.

Add the corn and milk to a food processor. Process until smooth and combined. Add the honey, butter and eggs to the food processor. Process until all the ingredients are combined.

In a mixing bowl, add the all purpose flour, oat bran flour, cornmeal, baking powder and salt. Stir until combined and add the corn mixture to the dry ingredients. Stir only until the batter is moistened and combined. Spoon the batter into the hot skillet.

Bake for 20 minutes or until a toothpick inserted in the center of the cornbread comes out clean. Remove the skillet from the oven and serve.

Cheesy Italian Corn Squares

Makes a 9 x 13 baking pan

1 1/4 cups all purpose flour
2 tbs. minced fresh parsley
1 tsp. baking soda
1 tsp. season salt
1/2 tsp. dried basil
1/2 tsp. dried oregano
1/2 tsp. black pepper
4 beaten eggs
2 cups whole kernel corn
1 cup ricotta cheese
1/3 cup finely chopped onion
1/4 cup freshly grated Parmesan cheese
1/4 cup vegetable oil
2 cups shredded mozzarella cheese
1 tsp. paprika

Preheat the oven to 350°. Spray a 9 x 13 baking pan with non stick cooking spray. In a mixing bowl, add the all purpose flour, parsley, baking soda, season salt, basil, oregano and black pepper. Stir until well combined. Add the eggs, corn, ricotta cheese, onion, Parmesan cheese, vegetable oil and 1 1/2 cups mozzarella cheese to the dry ingredients. Stir only until the batter is moistened and combined.

Spoon the batter into the prepared pan. Sprinkle 1/2 cup mozzarella cheese and the paprika over the top of the batter. Bake for 30 minutes or until the bread is done and golden brown. Remove the bread from the oven. Cut into small squares and serve.

Cheddar Lemon Corn Muffins

Makes 12 muffins

1 3/4 cups all purpose flour
3/4 cup shredded cheddar cheese
1/4 cup plain white or yellow cornmeal
1/4 cup granulated sugar
1/4 cup chopped almonds
2 tsp. baking powder
1/2 tsp. ground nutmeg
1/2 tsp. grated lemon zest
1/4 tsp. salt
1 egg
1 1/2 cups cooked whole kernel corn
1/4 cup vegetable oil
1/4 cup whole milk, optional

Preheat the oven to 375°. Spray a 12 count muffin tin with non stick cooking spray. In a mixing bowl, add the all purpose flour, cheddar cheese, cornmeal, granulated sugar, almonds, baking powder, nutmeg, lemon zest and salt. Whisk until well combined.

Add the egg, corn and vegetable oil to the dry ingredients. Mix only until the batter is moistened and combined. Depending upon the juiciness of your corn, you may need to add milk to make a creamy batter. Spoon the batter into the muffins cups filling them about 2/3 full.

Bake for 25 minutes or until a toothpick inserted in the center of the muffins comes out clean. Remove the muffins from the oven and cool the muffins in the pan for 10 minutes. Serve the muffins warm.

Corn Waffles with Cilantro Lime Butter

Makes 10 waffles

1 3/4 cups self rising flour
1/3 cup granulated sugar
1/2 tsp. salt
3 eggs, separated
1/2 cup whole milk
1/3 cup vegetable oil
1 cup frozen whole kernel corn, thawed
1/2 cup softened unsalted butter
1 tbs. chopped fresh cilantro
1 tsp. grated lime zest
1 tsp. fresh lime juice

In a mixing bowl, add the egg whites. Using a mixer on medium speed, beat the egg whites until stiff peaks form. In a separate mixing bowl, add the self rising flour, granulated sugar and salt. Whisk until combined.

In a mixing bowl, add the egg yolks, milk, corn and vegetable oil. Whisk until well combined and add to the dry ingredients. Mix only until the batter is moistened. Gently fold in the beaten egg whites.

Preheat your waffle iron. Spray the waffle iron with non stick cooking spray or a light brushing of vegetable oil. Pour about 1/4 cup batter onto the waffle iron. Cook for 3-4 minutes or until the waffles are golden brown. Repeat the process until all the waffles are cooked.

Use batter according to your waffle iron instructions. Some waffle irons may use more batter and others may use less. Cook the waffles according to your waffle iron instructions.

In a small bowl, add the softened butter, cilantro, lime zest and lime juice. Stir until well combined. Serve the butter over the hot waffles. Use the waffles as a side dish or as a main dish with taco meat or beans.

Roasted Corn and Lobster Beignets

Makes 8 appetizer servings

2 cups fresh corn kernels
3 tbs. vegetable oil
1 tsp. salt
1/2 tsp. black pepper
8 oz. bottle clam juice
1/3 cup dark amber beer
3/4 tsp. active dry yeast
1/2 cup whole milk
1 cup all purpose flour
2 tbs. unsalted butter
2 tbs. Tabasco sauce
1 cup finely chopped cooked lobster
3 eggs whites, at room temperature
Vegetable oil for frying

Preheat the oven to 400°. In a small bowl, add the corn, 2 tablespoons vegetable oil, 1/2 teaspoon salt and 1/4 teaspoon black pepper. Stir until the corn is coated in the oil and seasonings. Spread the corn, in a single layer, on a baking pan. Bake for 20 minutes or until the corn is tender and golden brown. Remove the corn from the oven.

In a small sauce pan over high heat, add the clam juice. Cook for 20 minutes or until the juice is reduced to about 1 tablespoon. Remove the pan from the heat. In a sauce pan over medium heat, add the beer. Cook until the temperature of the beer reaches 105° on a candy thermometer. Remove the pan from the heat and add the yeast to the beer. Let the yeast sit undisturbed for 5 minutes.

Add 1 tablespoon vegetable oil, 1/2 teaspoon salt, 1/4 teaspoon black pepper, corn, clam juice, milk, all purpose flour, butter, Tabasco sauce and lobster to the beer and yeast. Stir until all the ingredients are moistened and combined. Cover the pan with a lid and let the batter rise for 30 minutes.

Roasted Corn and Lobster Beignets cont'd

In a mixing bowl, add the egg whites. Using a mixer on medium speed, beat for 4 minutes or until stiff peaks form. Gently fold the egg whites into the batter.

In a deep fryer or large sauce pan over medium high heat, add vegetable oil to a depth of 2" in the pan. The temperature of the oil should be 360°. You will need to cook the beignets in batches. If you add too many beignets at one time to the oil, the temperature of the oil will drop and the beignets will be greasy.

Drop the beignets by teaspoonfuls into the hot oil. Cook for 2 minutes or until the beignets are golden brown. Remove the beignets from the hot oil and drain on paper towels.

Corn and Crab Fritters

Makes 10 servings

3 tbs. unsalted butter
1 1/2 cups fresh corn kernels
1/2 cup chopped red bell pepper
3 green onions, chopped
1 cup plain yellow cornmeal
1/2 cup all purpose flour
1 tsp. baking powder
1 tsp. baking soda
1 tsp. salt
1 tsp. black pepper
2 beaten eggs
1 cup ricotta cheese
1/2 cup buttermilk
1 tbs. fresh lime juice
1 lb. fresh lump crabmeat
Vegetable oil for frying

In a skillet over medium heat, add the butter. When the butter melts, add the corn, red bell pepper and green onions. Saute the corn for 8 minutes. Remove the skillet from the heat.

In a mixing bowl, add the cornmeal, all purpose flour, baking powder, baking soda, salt and black pepper. Stir until the dry ingredients are combined. Add the eggs, ricotta cheese, buttermilk and lime juice to the dry ingredients. Stir until the batter is moistened and combined. Gently fold in the corn mixture and crabmeat.

Using 1/4 cup batter, form the batter into patties. You will need to cook the fritters in batches. In a heavy skillet over medium high heat, add vegetable oil to a depth of 1/4" in the skillet. When the oil is hot, add the fritters. Cook for 3 minutes on each side or until they are golden brown. Remove the fritters from the oil and drain on paper towels. Add vegetable oil as needed until all the fritters are cooked.

4 SOUPS, SALADS & SIDES

Corn chowder, corn salads, savory corn puddings and of course corn on the cob dominate this section. You will find our favorite ways to use fresh corn from the garden or frozen and canned corn.

Corn and Asiago Bread Pudding

Makes 12 servings

1 1/2 cups whole milk
1 cup whipping cream
3 eggs
1/2 tsp. salt
1/2 tsp. black pepper
8 cups French bread, cubed
4 cups fresh corn kernels
1 1/2 cups shredded Asiago cheese

In a mixing bowl, add the milk, whipping cream, eggs, salt and black pepper. Whisk until all the ingredients are well combined. Add the bread to the mixing bowl and toss until the bread cubes are moistened. Let the pudding sit at room temperature for 30 minutes.

Preheat the oven to 375°. Add the corn and Asiago cheese to the bread cubes. Stir until combined. Spray a 9 x 13 baking dish with non stick cooking spray. Spoon the pudding into the baking dish. Bake for 45 minutes or until the pudding is set and golden brown. Do not over bake the pudding. The pudding needs to be moist but set in the center. Remove the pudding from the oven and cool for 5 minutes before serving.

Parmesan Corn Pudding

Makes 8 servings

4 cups fresh or frozen corn
1/3 cup granulated sugar
1/4 cup all purpose flour
2 tbs. plain yellow cornmeal
1/2 tsp. salt
6 tbs. unsalted butter, melted
1 1/2 cups whole milk
4 eggs
2 tbs. chopped fresh chives
1/2 cup shredded Parmesan cheese

Preheat the oven to 350°. Spray a 2 quart casserole dish with non stick cooking spray. In a food processor, add 2 cups corn, granulated sugar, all purpose flour, cornmeal, salt, butter, milk and eggs. Process until smooth and combined.

Spoon the mixture into a large mixing bowl. Add 2 cups corn, chives and Parmesan cheese. Stir until well combined and spoon into the prepared casserole dish. Bake for 45 minutes or until the pudding is set in the center. Remove the dish from the oven and serve.

Southern Corn Pudding

Makes 4 servings

3 eggs
1 cup whipping cream
4 cups cooked whole kernel corn
1/2 cup unsalted butter, melted
2 tbs. granulated sugar
4 1/2 tsp. all purpose flour
1 tsp. baking powder
1/2 tsp. salt
1/4 tsp. black pepper

Preheat the oven to 350°. Spray a 1 1/2 quart casserole dish with non stick cooking spray. In a mixing bowl, add the eggs and whipping cream. Whisk until smooth and combined. Add the corn and butter to the bowl. Whisk until combined.

Add the granulated sugar, all purpose flour, baking powder, salt and black pepper to the bowl. Whisk only until the dry ingredients are moistened and combined. Spoon the pudding into the baking dish. Bake for 45 minutes or until the center of the pudding is set and the pudding is golden brown. Remove the pudding from the oven and serve.

Green Chile Corn Pudding

Makes 8 servings

1/4 cup granulated sugar
3 tbs. all purpose flour
2 tsp. baking powder
1 1/2 tsp. salt
6 eggs
2 cups whipping cream
1/2 cup unsalted butter, melted
6 cups fresh or frozen whole kernel corn
1/2 tsp. ground cumin
4 oz. can diced green chiles

Spray a 9 x 13 baking dish with non stick cooking spray. Preheat the oven to 350°. In a mixing bowl, add the granulated sugar, all purpose flour, baking powder and salt. Stir until combined. In a separate mixing bowl, add the eggs, whipping cream and butter. Stir until all the ingredients are combined.

Continue whisking and slowly add the dry ingredients to the wet ingredients. Stir in the corn, green chiles with liquid and cumin. Mix only until the batter is moistened and combined. Spoon the batter into the prepared pan. Bake for 30 minutes or until the center of the pudding is set and the pudding is deep golden brown. Remove the pudding from the oven and serve.

Corn Chive Flan

Makes 6 servings

2 1/2 cups frozen whole kernel corn, thawed
1 1/2 cups whipping cream
4 eggs
3/4 tsp. salt
1/4 tsp. Tabasco sauce
3 tbs. shredded Monterey Jack cheese
1/3 cup chopped fresh chives
Hot water

In a blender, add the corn, whipping cream, eggs, salt and Tabasco sauce. Process until smooth. Turn the blender off and stir in the Monterey Jack cheese and chives.

Spray 6 eight ounce ramekins with non stick cooking spray. Preheat the oven to 325°. Spoon the flan into the ramekins. Place the ramekins in a deep roasting pan. Pour hot water to a 1" depth in the pan. Cover the pan with aluminum foil.

Bake for 45 minutes or until a knife inserted in the center of each dish comes out clean. Remove the pan from the oven and remove the ramekins from the pan. Invert the ramekins to remove the flan. Serve immediately.

Fiesta Corn Rice Casserole

Makes a 9 x 13 baking dish

2 cups uncooked long grain rice
6 cups water
2 tbs. unsalted butter
1 green bell pepper, chopped
1 onion, chopped
15 oz. can cream style corn
11 oz. can Mexican style corn, drained
10 oz. can diced tomatoes with green chiles
8 oz. Mexican Velveeta, cubed
1/2 tsp. salt
1/4 tsp. black pepper
1/2 cup shredded cheddar cheese

In a sauce pan over medium heat, add the water. When the water is at a full boil, stir in the rice. Bring the rice back to a boil. Reduce the heat to low and place a lid on the pan. Simmer the rice about 20 minutes or until the rice is tender. Remove the pan from the heat.

In a large skillet over medium heat, add the butter, green bell pepper and onion. Saute the vegetables for 5 minutes. Stir in the rice, cream style corn, Mexican corn, diced tomatoes with liquid, Mexican Velveeta, salt and black pepper. Stir until combined and the cheese melts. Remove the skillet from the heat.

Preheat the oven to 350°. Spray a 9 x 13 baking dish with non stick cooking spray. Spoon the mixture into the casserole dish. Bake for 30 minutes. The dish should be hot and bubbly. Sprinkle the cheddar cheese over the top and bake for 5 minutes. Remove the dish from the oven and serve.

Green Bean & Corn Casserole

Makes 6 servings

2 cups cooked green beans
2 cups cooked whole kernel corn
10.75 oz. can cream of celery soup
3 celery ribs, chopped
1/2 cup chopped onion
1/2 cup shredded cheddar cheese
1 cup sour cream
1/4 tsp. salt
1/4 tsp. black pepper
22 round butter crackers, crushed
1/4 cup unsalted butter, melted

Add the green beans, corn, cream of celery soup, celery, onion, cheddar cheese, sour cream, salt and black pepper to a mixing bowl. Stir until all the ingredients are combined.

Spray a 11 x 7 casserole dish with non stick cooking spray. Preheat the oven to 350°. Spoon the casserole into the dish. Sprinkle the crackers over the top of the casserole. Drizzle the butter over the crackers.

Bake for 30 minutes or until the casserole is hot and bubbly. Remove the dish from the oven and serve.

Creamy Corn & Broccoli Side Dish

Makes 8 servings

16 oz. pkg. frozen cut broccoli
16 oz. pkg. frozen whole kernel corn
10.75 oz. can cream of chicken soup
1 cup shredded American cheese
1/2 cup shredded cheddar cheese
1/4 cup whole milk

Spray a 4 quart slow cooker with non stick cooking spray. Add all the ingredients to the slow cooker. Stir until combined. Set the temperature to low and cook for 5 hours. Stir the side dish before serving.

Tex Mex Rice & Corn

Makes 8 servings

1/2 cup chopped onion
1/2 cup chopped green bell pepper
2 tsp. olive oil
2 garlic cloves, minced
1 cup dry long grain rice
1 cup chunky salsa
1 3/4 cups chicken broth
1 cup fresh or frozen whole kernel corn
1 tsp. instant chicken bouillon granules
1/4 tsp. black pepper

In a sauce pan over medium heat, add the onion, green bell pepper and olive oil. Saute the vegetables for 5 minutes. Add the garlic and saute the garlic for 1 minute. Add the rice and salsa to the pan. Saute the rice for 3 minutes.

Add the chicken broth, corn, chicken bouillon granules and black pepper to the pan. Bring the rice to a boil and reduce the heat to low. Place a lid on the pan and simmer the rice for 15 minutes or until the rice and corn are tender. Remove the pan from the heat and let the rice sit for 5 minutes. Remove the lid from the pan and fluff the rice with a fork before serving.

Company Corn

Makes 6 servings

4 cups fresh or frozen whole kernel corn
1 cup chopped onion
1/4 cup chopped celery
1/3 cup unsalted butter, cubed
2 tbs. minced fresh parsley
1 tsp. salt
1/2 tsp. dried savory
1/2 tsp. black pepper
3/4 cup sour cream
1 tsp. fresh lemon juice

In a sauce pan over medium heat, add the corn. Cover the corn with water and bring the corn to a boil. Cook for 6 minutes or until the corn is tender. Remove the pan from the heat and drain all the water from the corn.

In a skillet over medium heat, add the onion, celery and butter. Saute the onion and celery for 5 minutes or until the vegetables are tender. Add the parsley, salt, savory and black pepper to the skillet. Stir until combined.

Add the corn, sour cream and lemon juice to the skillet. Stir until combined. Cook only until the corn is thoroughly heated. Do not let the corn boil once you add the sour cream. Remove the skillet from the heat and serve.

Cayenne Corn

Makes 4 servings

1/4 cup chopped onion
1/4 cup chopped green bell pepper
1 tbs. unsalted butter
2 cups fresh or thawed frozen whole kernel corn
1/2 cup diced fresh tomato
1 tsp. salt
1/8 tsp. black pepper
1/4 tsp. cayenne pepper

In a sauce pan over medium heat, add the onion, green bell pepper, butter and corn. Saute the corn and vegetables for 8 minutes or until the corn is tender. Add the tomato, salt, black pepper and cayenne pepper. Stir constantly and cook for 3 minutes. Remove the pan from the heat and serve.

Southern Cream Corn

Makes 8 servings

8 ears fresh corn
2 tbs. all purpose flour
2 tbs. granulated sugar
1 tsp. salt
1/2 cup whole milk
1/4 cup plus 2 tbs. unsalted butter
1/2 cup heavy cream

Remove the husks and silk from the corn. Cut the corn from the cob, scraping the cob to remove the pulp.

In a small bowl, add the all purpose flour, granulated sugar and salt. Stir until the dry ingredients are combined. Gradually stir in the milk and mix until the batter is smooth.

In a cast iron skillet, add the butter. When the butter has melted, stir in the corn. Slowly stir in the flour mixture. Cover the skillet and bring the corn to a boil. Reduce the heat to low and simmer for 15 minutes. You will have to stir often to keep the corn from burning and sticking to the pan. When the corn is tender, stir in the heavy cream. Remove the skillet from the heat. Serve immediately.

Corn & Zucchini Skillet

Makes 4 servings

3/4 cup chopped onion
3 tbs. olive oil
2 garlic cloves, minced
3 zucchini, quartered lengthwise and sliced
1 tomato, seeded and chopped
2 cups cooked whole kernel corn
1/4 cup water
1 tbs. dried parsley flakes
1/4 tsp. salt
1/4 tsp. black pepper
1/2 cup shredded cheddar cheese

In a large skillet over medium heat, add the onion and olive oil. Saute the onion for 5 minutes or until the onion is tender. Add the garlic and saute the garlic for 1 minute. Add the zucchini and tomato to the skillet. Saute the vegetables for 5 minutes.

Add the corn, water, parsley, salt and black pepper. Stir until all the ingredients are combined. Bring the corn to a boil and reduce the heat to low. Stir occasionally and cook for 10 minutes. Sprinkle the cheddar cheese over the vegetables and remove the skillet from the heat. Serve hot.

Roasted Corn & Garlic Chipotle Mashed Potatoes

Makes 6 servings

1 head garlic
2 tbs. vegetable oil
3 ears fresh corn, husked
4 cups red potatoes, peeled and cut into 1/2" cubes
3/4 cup sour cream
1/2 cup unsalted butter
1/2 cup whole milk
1 1/2 tsp. salt
1 canned chipotle pepper in adobo sauce, minced
1 tsp. adobe sauce from canned chipotle pepper
1 tsp. black pepper
1/2 cup chopped fresh cilantro

Cut a thin slice off the top of the garlic head. Place the garlic on a piece of aluminum foil. Drizzle 1 tablespoon vegetable oil over the garlic. Wrap the garlic in the aluminum foil. Brush 1 tablespoon vegetable oil over the ears of corn. Place the corn and garlic on a baking sheet. Preheat the oven to 400°. Bake for 45 minutes or until the corn is golden brown. Remove the pan from the oven. Cool the garlic and corn for 10 minutes.

Remove the corn kernels from the cob and set aside. Squeeze the garlic cloves into a small bowl. In a sauce pan over medium heat, add the potatoes. Cover the potatoes with water and bring the potatoes to a boil. Simmer the potatoes for 10 minutes or until they are tender. Remove the pan from the heat and drain all the water from the potatoes.

In a sauce pan over medium heat, add the roasted garlic cloves, sour cream, butter, milk, salt, chipotle pepper, adobo sauce and black pepper. Stir constantly and cook until the butter melts and all the ingredients are combined. Do not let the sour cream boil. Remove the pan from the heat.

Add the potatoes to a serving bowl. Using a potato masher, mash the potatoes. Add the sour cream mixture from the pan. Stir until the potatoes are creamy. Add the corn and cilantro to the potatoes. Stir until all the ingredients are combined and serve.

Swiss Corn Bake

Makes 8 servings

6 ears fresh corn
1/2 cup water
1 egg, beaten
1 cup Swiss cheese
5 oz. can evaporated milk
2 tbs. finely chopped onion
1/2 tsp. salt
1/4 tsp. black pepper
1 tsp. unsalted butter, melted
1/2 cup soft bread crumbs

Remove the husks and silk from the corn. Cut the corn from the cob scraping the cob to remove the pulp. In a sauce pan over medium heat, add the corn and water. Bring the corn to a boil and reduce the heat to medium low. Simmer for 5 minutes. Stir often or the corn will stick to the pan. Remove the pan from the heat and drain any liquid from the corn.

Preheat the oven to 350°. Spray a 9 x 11 casserole dish with non stick cooking spray. Add the egg, 1/2 cup Swiss cheese, evaporated milk, onion, salt and black pepper to the corn. Stir well to combine the ingredients. Spoon the corn mixture into the baking dish.

In a small bowl, combine the bread crumbs and the melted butter. Sprinkle the remaining 1/2 cup cheese over the corn mixture. Top the cheese with the bread crumbs. Bake for 25 minutes or until the corn is tender and the casserole is hot. Remove the dish from the oven and serve.

Creamy Sweet Corn

Makes 4 servings

2 cups fresh corn kernels
1/4 cup half and half
2 tbs. unsalted butter
1 tbs. granulated sugar
1/2 tsp. salt

Add all the ingredients to a sauce pan over medium heat. Stir until combined and bring the corn to a boil. When the corn is boiling, reduce the heat to low. Simmer for 8 minutes or until the corn is tender. Remove the pan from the heat and serve.

Southern Fried Corn

Makes 4 servings

3 tbs. unsalted butter
4 cups fresh corn kernels
1 tsp. granulated sugar
1/2 tsp. salt
1/2 tsp. black pepper

In a cast iron skillet over medium heat, add the butter. When the butter melts, add the corn kernels. Saute the corn for 10 minutes or until the corn is tender. Add the granulated sugar, salt and black pepper to the skillet. Stir constantly and cook for 1 minute. Remove the skillet from the heat and serve.

Buttermilk Fried Corn

Makes 3 cups

3 cups fresh corn kernels
2 1/4 cups buttermilk
1 cup all purpose flour
1 cup plain white or yellow cornmeal
1 tsp. salt
1 1/2 tsp. black pepper
Vegetable oil for frying

In a mixing bowl, add the corn and buttermilk. Stir until combined and let the corn sit at room temperature for 30 minutes. Drain all the buttermilk from the corn.

In a Ziploc bag, add the all purpose flour, cornmeal, salt and black pepper. Close the bag and shake until all the ingredients are combined. Add the corn to the bag. Close the bag and shake until the corn is coated in the dry ingredients.

In a dutch oven over high heat, add vegetable oil to a depth of 1" in the pan. The temperature of the oil should be 375°. You will need to fry the corn in batches. If you add too much corn to the hot oil, the temperature of the oil will drop and the corn will be greasy.

Add about 3/4 cup corn to the hot oil. Fry for 2 minutes or until the corn is golden brown. Remove the corn from the hot oil and drain on paper towels. Add vegetable oil as needed after each batch to maintain a 1" depth in the pan. Serve hot.

Spicy Baked Pepper Corn

Makes 6 servings

8 oz. cream cheese, cubed
1/3 cup unsalted butter
1/2 cup diced green bell pepper
1/2 cup diced red bell pepper
2 jalapeno peppers, seeded and diced
4 cups fresh or frozen whole kernel corn
Salt and black pepper to season

Preheat the oven to 350°. In a sauce pan over medium heat, add the cream cheese and butter. Stir constantly and cook until the butter and cream cheese melt. Remove the pan from the heat and stir in the green bell pepper, red bell pepper, jalapeno peppers and corn.

Spoon the corn into an 8" square baking dish. Bake for 20 minutes or until the corn and peppers are tender. Remove the dish from the oven and season to taste with salt and black pepper before serving.

Cheesy Corn Bake

Makes 8 servings

2 tbs. unsalted butter
4 tsp. all purpose flour
1/8 tsp. garlic powder
3/4 cup whole milk
1 1/2 cups shredded sharp cheddar cheese
3 oz. pkg. cream cheese, cubed
6 cups fresh or frozen whole kernel corn
2/3 cup diced cooked ham

In a sauce pan over low heat, add the butter. When the butter melts, add the all purpose flour and garlic powder. Stir constantly and cook for 1 minute. Add the milk and cook until the sauce thickens and bubbles. Remove the pan from the heat.

Add the cheddar cheese, cream cheese, corn and ham to the pan. Stir until well combined. Spray a 2 quart casserole dish with non stick cooking spray. Spoon the corn into the dish. Preheat the oven to 350°. Bake for 45 minutes. Remove the dish from the oven and serve.

Corn Stuffed Zucchini

Makes 4 servings

2 medium zucchini, halved
3 tbs. unsalted butter, melted
1/3 cup chopped onion
1/3 cup chopped green bell pepper
1 1/2 cups whole kernel corn, cooked
1 tsp. dried tarragon, crushed
1/4 tsp. black pepper
Salt to taste

Preheat the oven to 350°. Cut the zucchini in half lengthwise. Scoop out the pulp from each zucchini leaving about a 1/4" thick shell. Place the zucchini pulp in a mixing bowl.

Add the butter, onion, green bell pepper, corn, tarragon and black pepper to the bowl. Stir until well combined. Season to taste with salt. Spoon the mixture into the zucchini shells. Place the shells on a baking sheet. Bake for 25-30 minutes or until the zucchini shells are hot and tender. Remove the zucchini from the oven and serve.

Ancho Chili Corn

Makes 4 servings

2 cups fresh corn kernels
1 tbs. vegetable oil
1 cup diced fresh tomatoes
4 tbs. minced onion
1/2 ancho chile pepper, chopped
4 tbs. unsalted butter
1/2 cup chicken broth
2 tsp. chopped fresh cilantro
1/2 tsp. salt
1/2 tsp. black pepper

In a skillet over medium heat, add the vegetable oil. When the oil is hot, add the corn. Stir constantly and cook for 5 minutes. Add the tomatoes, onion, ancho chile pepper, butter, chicken broth, cilantro, salt and black pepper.

Stir until all the ingredients are combined. Reduce the heat to low. Stir frequently and cook for 3 minutes or until the corn is tender. Remove the skillet from the heat and serve.

Grilled Southwestern Corn

Makes 4 servings

4 ears fresh corn, husked
1/4 tsp. salt
2 tsp. finely chopped fresh cilantro
1 tbs. olive oil
1/4 tsp. ground cumin
1/8 tsp. garlic powder
1/8 tsp. cayenne pepper

Have your grill hot and ready. Place the corn on the grill and cook about 10 minutes or until the corn is tender. Turn the corn frequently so all sides cook evenly.

While the corn is cooking, make the glaze. In a small skillet over medium heat, add the salt, cilantro, olive oil, cumin, garlic powder and cayenne pepper. Stir until combined and cook only until the glaze and spices are heated. Remove the skillet from the heat. Remove the corn from the grill. Brush the glaze over the corn and serve.

Chili Lime Grilled Corn

Makes 8 servings

8 ears fresh corn
1/2 cup softened butter
1 tsp. grated lime zest
1 tsp. fresh lime juice
Chili powder to taste

Pull back the husk from the corn but do not totally remove the husk from the corn. Remove the silk from the corn. Pull the husk back over the corn ears. Place the ears of corn in a large pot. Cover the corn with water. Let the husk soak for 1 hour.

Drain all the water from the corn and pat the corn dry with paper towels. In a small bowl, add the butter, lime zest, lime juice and chili powder to taste. Stir until combined and let the butter sit at room temperature while you cook the corn.

Have your grill hot and ready. Place the corn on the grill. Close the lid and cook for 25 minutes or until the corn is tender. Turn the corn often so the corn cooks evenly. Remove the corn from the grill.

Carefully remove the husk and spread the butter all over the corn. Serve hot.

Baked Indian Corn

You may never fix corn on the cob any other way. This makes a lot but it is delicious the next day too!

Makes 12 servings

12 ears fresh corn
1 lb. unsalted butter, softened
1/2 cup grated Parmesan cheese
1/2 teaspoon dried basil, crushed
1 tsp. salt
1 envelope dry chili cheese dip mix or chili seasoning mix

First you need to make the two different butters for the corn. In a small bowl, add half the butter, 1/2 cup Parmesan cheese, basil and salt. Stir until well combined.

In a separate bowl, add the remaining half of the butter and the chili cheese dip mix. Stir until well combined.

Peel the husk back from the corn, but do not remove the husk, leaving the stub on the corn. Remove all the silk. Generously spread whichever one of the butters you want on the corn. Pull the husks back up on the corn.

Preheat the oven to 400°. Wrap each ear of corn in heavy duty aluminum foil. Place the corn on a baking sheet. Bake for 25-30 minutes or until the corn is tender. Turn frequently so the corn cooks evenly. Remove the corn from the oven and spread the remaining butter on the corn before serving.

Cream Cheese Baked Corn on the Cob

Makes 6 servings

6 ears fresh corn, husked and silk removed
4 oz. container whipped cream cheese with chives
1/4 cup unsalted butter, softened
1/4 tsp salt
1/8 tsp. black pepper

In a small bowl, add the cream cheese, butter, salt and black pepper. Stir until well combined. Place each ear of corn on a piece of aluminum foil. Spread a tablespoon of the butter and cream cheese mixture over each ear of corn. Fold the aluminum foil around the corn.

Preheat the oven to 400°. Place the foil wrapped corn on a baking sheet. Bake for 45 minutes or until the corn is tender. Remove the corn from the oven and cool in the foil for 10 minutes. Remove the corn from the foil and spread the remaining butter and cream cheese over the corn before serving.

Grilled Corn with Red Chile Paste

Makes 1 cup

6 dried ancho peppers
4 cups water
1 red bell pepper, chopped
2 garlic cloves, minced
1 tsp. dried oregano
1 tsp. paprika
1 tsp. ground cumin
1 tsp. salt
2 tbs. cider vinegar
1 tbs. olive oil
2 cups cubed sourdough bread
6 ears fresh corn, husked

In a sauce pan over medium heat, add the ancho peppers and water. Bring the peppers to a boil and cook for 15 minutes. Remove the pan from the heat and drain the water from the peppers. Cool the peppers for 10 minutes.

Remove the stems and seeds from the peppers. Add the ancho peppers, red bell pepper, garlic, oregano, paprika, cumin and salt to a food processor. Process until the peppers are chopped. Add the cider vinegar, olive oil and sourdough bread to the food processor. Process until the paste is smooth and combined.

Have your grill hot and ready. Place the corn on the grill and cook for 15 minutes or until the corn is tender. Turn the corn frequently so the corn cooks evenly. Remove the corn from the grill and brush the red chile paste over the hot corn before serving.

Grilled Corn with Jalapeno Lime Butter

Makes 10 servings

3/4 cup unsalted butter, softened
2 jalapeno peppers, seeded and minced
2 tbs. grated lime zest
1 tsp. fresh lime juice
10 ears fresh corn, husked
2 tbs. olive oil
1 tbs. salt
1 tsp. black pepper

In a small bowl, add the butter, jalapeno peppers, lime zest and lime juice. Stir until well combined. Place the butter on a piece of plastic wrap. Form the butter into a log. Wrap the butter in plastic wrap and chill for 1 hour.

Brush the olive oil over the corn. Sprinkle the salt and black pepper over the corn. Have your grill hot and ready. Place the corn on the grill. Cook for 10-15 minutes or until the corn is tender. Turn the corn often so all sides cook evenly. Remove the corn from the grill and spread the butter over the corn before serving.

Grilled Garlic Chive Corn on the Cob

Makes 6 servings

6 ears fresh corn
1/2 cup unsalted butter, softened
2 garlic cloves, minced
1/4 cup minced fresh chives

Pull back the husk from the corn but do not remove the husk. Remove the silk from the corn. Pull the husk back up over the corn. Place the corn in a large bowl. Cover the corn with cold water. Soak the corn for 1 hour. You must soak the husk or they will burn on the grill.

In a small bowl, add the butter, garlic and chives. Stir until combined. Have your grill hot and ready. Remove the corn from the water and place on the grill. Close the grill lid and cook about 20 minutes or until the corn is tender. Turn the corn frequently so all sides cook evenly. Remove the corn from the grill.

Remove the husk from the corn. The corn will be hot so be careful when removing the husk. Spread the butter over the corn and serve.

Grilled Corn with Maple Vinaigrette

Makes 6 servings

6 ears fresh corn with husks
1/4 cup unsweetened brewed tea
1/4 cup vegetable oil
3 tbs. balsamic vinegar
2 tbs. maple syrup
1/4 tsp. salt
1/4 tsp. black pepper

Pull back the husk from the corn but do not remove the husk. Remove the silk from the corn. Pull the husk back up over the corn. Place the corn in a large bowl. Cover the corn with cold water. Soak the corn for 1 hour. You must soak the husk or they will burn on the grill.

Have your grill hot and ready. Remove the corn from the water and place on the grill. Close the grill lid and cook about 20 minutes or until the corn is tender. Turn the corn frequently so all sides cook evenly. Remove the corn from the grill. Let the corn cool while you prepare the vinaigrette.

In a small bowl, add the tea, vegetable oil, balsamic vinegar, maple syrup, salt and black pepper. Stir until well combined. Remove the husk from the corn. The corn will be hot so be careful when removing the husk. Spread the vinaigrette all over the corn and serve.

Creole Grilled Corn

Makes 6 servings

6 ears fresh corn, husked
1/4 cup unsalted butter
1 tsp. dried basil
1 tsp. Tabasco sauce
1/2 tsp. Creole seasoning
1/4 tsp. black pepper

Have your grill hot and ready. Place the corn on the grill. Cook for 5 minutes. In a sauce pan over medium heat, add the butter, basil, Tabasco sauce, Creole seasoning and black pepper. Stir constantly and cook until the butter melts. Remove the pan from the heat.

Brush the butter on the corn and cook for 5 minutes or until the corn is tender. Remove the corn from the grill. Brush any remaining butter over the corn and serve.

Grilled Corn with Creamy Chipotle Sauce

Makes 8 servings

2 garlic cloves, peeled
1 canned chipotle pepper in adobo sauce
1/2 tsp. salt
1 cup cottage cheese
1/4 cup fresh cilantro leaves
1/4 cup mayonnaise
1/4 cup plain yogurt
2 tsp. adobo sauce from canned chipotle
8 ears fresh corn, husked

In a blender, add the garlic, chipotle pepper, salt, cottage cheese, cilantro, mayonnaise, yogurt and adobo sauce. Process until smooth and combined. Spoon the sauce into a bowl and cover the bowl. Refrigerate at least 12 hours before serving.

Have your grill hot and ready. Spray the grill with non stick cooking spray. Place the corn on the grill. Turn frequently and cook for 10 minutes or until the corn is tender. Remove the corn from the grill and brush the sauce over the corn before serving.

Smoked Thyme Butter Corn

Makes 8 servings

Hickory wood chips
1/2 cup unsalted butter
2 tbs. chopped fresh thyme
8 ears fresh corn

Soak the hickory chips in water at least 30 minutes. Prepare a charcoal fire in your smoker and let the charcoal burn off about 20 minutes.

In a small bowl, add the butter and thyme. Remove the husk and silk from the corn. Spread the butter on the corn. Place the hickory chips in the smoker and fill the water pan. Place the corn on the cooking grate. Smoke for 30 minutes or until the corn is tender. Remove the corn from the smoker and serve.

Grilled Sweet Corn & Peppers

Makes 6 servings

1 red bell pepper, thinly sliced
1 green bell pepper, thinly sliced
1 jalapeno pepper, seeded and thinly sliced
1 onion, cut into thin wedges
1/2 tsp. salt
1/2 tsp. black pepper
1/8 tsp. cayenne pepper
6 ears fresh corn, husk removed

Have your grill hot and ready. Cut each ear of corn in half. Add the red bell pepper, green bell pepper, jalapeno pepper, salt, black pepper, onion, cayenne pepper and corn to a large grill pan. Toss until all the ingredients are combined.

Place the pan on the grill. Close the grill lid and cook for 20 minutes or until the corn is tender. Stir the vegetables occasionally while cooking. Remove the pan from the grill and serve.

Garlic Pepper Corn

Makes 8 servings

1 tbs. dried parsley flakes
1 tbs. garlic pepper seasoning
1/2 tsp. paprika
1/4 tsp. salt
8 fresh ears corn, husked
1/4 cup melted unsalted butter

In a small bowl, add the parsley flakes, garlic pepper seasoning, paprika and salt. Stir until combined. Place the corn in a large dutch oven over medium high heat. Cover the corn with water and bring the corn to a boil. Place a lid on the pan and cook for 4 minutes or until the corn is tender. Remove the corn from the heat and drain all the water from the corn.

Brush the corn with melted butter. Sprinkle the parsley seasoning over the corn and serve.

Bacon and Caramelized Onion Corn

Makes 4 servings

6 bacon slices, chopped
2 onions, cut into thin strips
4 cups fresh corn kernels
2 tbs. light molasses
1/4 tsp. salt
1/4 tsp. black pepper

In a cast iron skillet, add the bacon. Cook for 6 minutes or until the bacon is crispy. Remove the bacon from the skillet and drain on paper towels. Add the onions to the bacon drippings in the skillet. Saute the onions for 15 minutes or until they are tender and golden brown.

Add the corn to the skillet. Stir frequently and cook for 8 minutes or until the corn is tender. Add the molasses, salt, black pepper and bacon to the skillet. Stir until combined and cook for 1 minute. Remove the skillet from the heat and serve.

Grilled Chili Bacon Corn

Makes 8 servings

8 ears fresh corn, husked
8 bacon slices
2 tbs. chili powder

Have your grill hot and ready. Wrap a bacon slice around each ear of corn. Sprinkle the chili powder over the corn and bacon. Wrap each ear of corn in heavy duty aluminum foil.

Place the corn on the grill and cook about 20 minutes or until the corn is tender and the bacon cooked. Remove the corn from the grill. Cool the corn for 5 minutes before removing the aluminum foil. Carefully remove the foil as steam may escape and cause a severe burn. Serve immediately.

Field Peas, Corn & Okra

Makes 6 servings

2 celery ribs, sliced
1 1/2 cups diced onion
1/2 cup diced green bell pepper
1 garlic clove, minced
1 tbs. olive oil
1 tbs. Worcestershire sauce
2 tsp. Creole seasoning
1 tsp. black pepper
1 tsp. Tabasco sauce
1/2 tsp. salt
2 1/4 cups chicken broth
16 oz. pkg. frozen field peas with snaps
16 oz. pkg. sliced okra
2 cups fresh whole kernel corn

In a dutch oven over medium heat, add the celery, onion, green bell pepper, garlic and olive oil. Saute the vegetables for 8 minutes or until they are tender. Add the Worcestershire sauce, Creole seasoning, black pepper, Tabasco sauce and salt. Stir until all the ingredients are combined and cook for 1 minute.

Add the chicken broth to the pan. Bring the broth to a boil and add the field peas. Bring the peas to a boil and reduce the heat to low. Place a lid on the pan and simmer the peas for 25 minutes.

Add the okra and corn to the pan. Stir until all the ingredients are combined. Place the lid back on the pan and simmer for 12 minutes or until the vegetables are tender. Add no more than 1/2 cup water if needed to cook the vegetables. Remove the pan from the heat and serve.

Barbecued Corn

Makes 6 servings

4 cups whole kernel corn, cooked
1/4 cup thinly sliced green onion
3 tbs. barbecue sauce
1 tbs. yellow prepared mustard

In a sauce pan, add the corn, onion, barbecue sauce and mustard. Stir constantly and cook over medium heat for 5 minutes. Remove the pan from the heat and serve.

Sunshine Casserole

Makes 6 servings

2 cups finely shredded carrots
2 cups cooked rice
2 eggs, beaten
1 1/2 cups Velveeta cheese, diced
15 oz. can cream style corn
1/4 cup whole milk
1 tbs. unsalted butter, melted
1 tbs. dried minced onion
1/2 tsp. salt
1/4 tsp. black pepper

Preheat the oven to 350°. Spray a 2 quart casserole dish with non stick cooking spray. Add all the ingredients to the casserole dish. Stir until well combined. Bake for 35-45 minutes or until the casserole is hot and bubbly.

Scalloped Corn and Potatoes

Makes 4 servings

2 cups whole kernel corn, cooked
10 oz. can condensed cream of potato soup
1/4 tsp. salt
1/8 tsp. black pepper
2 tbs. unsalted butter, cut into small pieces
1/4 cup grated Parmesan cheese
Salt and black pepper to taste

Preheat the oven to 325°. Spray a 2 quart casserole dish with non stick cooking spray. Add the corn, potato soup, salt and black pepper to the casserole dish. Stir until well combined. Place the butter pieces over the top of the dish. Sprinkle the Parmesan cheese over the top of the casserole.

Bake for 20-25 minutes or until the casserole is hot, bubbly and set. Season with additional salt and black pepper if desired. A dash of cayenne pepper is also good in this casserole.

Fresh Corn Vinaigrette

Makes 1 1/2 cups

1 cup fresh corn kernels
2/3 cup olive oil
1/4 cup fresh lemon juice
1 garlic clove, minced
2 tbs. balsamic vinegar
1 tbs. Creole mustard
1 tsp. chopped fresh thyme
Salt and black pepper to taste

Add the corn, olive oil, lemon juice, garlic, balsamic vinegar, Creole mustard and thyme to a mixing bowl. Whisk until well combined. Season to taste with salt and black pepper. Serve over green salads, shrimp, fish or grilled chicken.

Barley Corn Salad

Makes 5 cups

1 cup dry quick cooking barley
1 1/4 cups fresh or frozen whole kernel corn
1/2 cup diced red bell pepper
1/2 cup chopped green bell pepper
1/2 cup sliced green onion
1/4 cup olive oil
1/4 cup lemon juice
1/4 cup chopped fresh cilantro
1/2 tsp. salt
Black pepper to taste

In a sauce pan over medium heat, add the barley. Cover the barley with water and cook for 5 minutes. Add the corn and cook for 5 minutes or until the corn and barley are tender. Remove the pan from the heat and drain all the water from the pan. Rinse the corn and barley with cold water until chilled. Drain all the water from the barley and corn.

Add the barley and corn to a serving bowl. Add the red bell pepper, green bell pepper and green onion to the bowl. In a jar with a lid, add the olive oil, lemon juice, cilantro and salt. Place the lid on the jar and shake until well combined. Pour the dressing over the corn and barley. Toss until all ingredients are combined. Season to taste with black pepper and serve.

Marinated Zucchini Corn Salad

Makes 6 servings

1/4 cup vegetable oil
1/4 cup cider vinegar
1/2 tsp. salt
1/2 tsp. black pepper
1/4 tsp. granulated sugar
1 1/2 cups thinly sliced zucchini
1 cup chopped onion
2 cups cooked whole kernel corn
1/4 cup minced red bell pepper

In a mixing bowl, add the vegetable oil, cider vinegar, salt, black pepper and granulated sugar. Whisk until the dressing is well combined. Add the zucchini, onion, corn and red bell pepper. Toss until all the ingredients are coated in the dressing. Cover the bowl and chill for 8 hours before serving.

Grilled Avocado Corn Poblano Salad

Makes 6 servings

6 small ears fresh corn, husked
2 poblano peppers
2 tbs. olive oil
1/2 tsp. grated lime zest
1/4 cup fresh lime juice
1/2 tsp. salt
1/4 tsp. black pepper
1/4 tsp. ground cumin
4 small avocados, peeled and chopped
1/2 cup chopped purple onion
3 tbs. chopped fresh cilantro

Spray the corn and poblano peppers with non stick cooking spray. Have your grill hot and ready. Place the corn and peppers on the grill. Close the grill lid and cook for 10 minutes. Turn the corn and peppers frequently so all sides cook evenly. Cook until the corn and peppers begin to char. Remove the vegetables from the grill and cool for 10 minutes.

Cut the corn from the cob. Seed and dice the poblano peppers. Add the corn, poblano peppers, purple onion, avocados and cilantro to a serving bowl. In a small bowl, add the olive oil, lime zest, lime juice, salt, black pepper and cumin. Whisk until combined and pour over the vegetables. Toss until the vegetables are coated in the dressing. Serve chilled or warm.

Grilled Italian Corn Salad

Makes 8 servings

3 cups prepared Italian salad dressing
8 large ears fresh corn, husked
4 green bell peppers, julienned
4 red bell peppers, julienned
2 purple onions, thinly sliced

Place the Italian salad dressing in a large Ziploc bag. Add the corn, green bell peppers, red bell peppers and purple onions. Close the bag and shake until all the vegetables are coated in the dressing. Refrigerate the vegetables for 30 minutes.

Remove the vegetables from the refrigerator. Have your grill hot and ready. Place the corn and vegetables in a cast iron skillet or grill pan. Do not discard the dressing. Place the vegetables on the grill. Close the lid and cook for 30 minutes or until the corn is tender. Remove the vegetables from the grill and cool for 5 minutes.

Remove the corn from the cob. Separate the onion into rings. Place the corn, peppers and onions in a bowl. Drizzle the remaining dressing over the salad if desired. Toss until combined and serve the salad warm.

Roasted Corn and Black Bean Salad

Makes 8 servings

2 cups fresh corn kernels
15 oz. can black beans, rinsed and drained
1 cup chopped tomato
1/3 cup lime juice
1/4 cup chopped purple onion
1 tbs. chopped jalapeno pepper
2 tbs. chopped fresh cilantro
2 tsp. Tabasco sauce
1/2 tsp. salt
1/2 tsp. ground cumin
1/2 tsp. ground coriander
1/2 tsp. black pepper

Turn the oven to the broiler position. Line a baking sheet with aluminum foil. Spread the corn over the baking sheet. Broil for 10 minutes or until the corn is lightly browned. Remove the corn from the oven and cool for 10 minutes.

Add the corn, black beans, tomato, lime juice, purple onion, jalapeno pepper, cilantro, Tabasco sauce, salt, cumin, coriander and black pepper to a serving bowl. Toss until all the ingredients are combined. Cover the bowl and chill for 4 hours before serving.

Fresh Corn Salad

Makes 10 servings

8 ears fresh corn, husked
1/2 cup vegetable oil
1/4 cup cider vinegar
1 1/2 tsp. lemon juice
1/4 cup minced fresh parsley
2 tsp. granulated sugar
1 tsp. salt
1/2 tsp. dried basil
1/4 tsp. cayenne pepper
2 cups diced tomatoes
1/2 cup chopped onion
1/3 cup chopped green bell pepper
1/3 cup chopped red bell pepper

In a large sauce pan over medium heat, add the corn. Cover the corn with water and bring the corn to a boil. Cook for 8 minutes or until the corn is tender. Remove the pan from the heat and drain all the water from the corn. Cool the corn for 10 minutes.

In a mixing bowl, add the vegetable oil, cider vinegar, lemon juice, parsley, granulated sugar, salt, basil and cayenne pepper. Whisk until well combined. Cut the corn from the cob and add to the bowl. Add the tomatoes, onion, green bell pepper and red bell pepper. Toss until all the ingredients are combined.

Cover the bowl and chill at least 6 hours before serving.

Taco Corn Salad

Makes 6 servings

2 tbs. taco seasoning mix
1/4 cup water
1/4 cup vegetable oil
2 cups cooked whole kernel corn
1 1/2 cups fresh tomato, diced
1/2 cup sliced black olives
1/4 cup diced green bell pepper

In a large bowl, add the taco seasoning mix, water and vegetable oil. Stir until well combined. Add the corn, tomato, black olives and green bell pepper. Toss to coat the vegetables with the dressing. Refrigerate for 1 hour before serving.

Creamy Corn Salad

Makes 4 servings

2 cups cooked whole kernel corn
1 cup diced and seeded tomato
2 tbs. chopped onion
1/3 cup mayonnaise
1/4 tsp. dried dill

Add all the ingredients to a serving bowl. Toss until combined. Cover the bowl and chill for 1 hour before serving.

Crunchy Corn Salad

Makes 8 servings

4 cups cooked whole kernel corn
2 cups grated cheddar cheese
1 cup mayonnaise
1 cup green bell pepper, chopped
1/2 cup purple onion, chopped
10 oz. bag chili cheese corn chips, crushed

In a serving bowl, add the corn, cheddar cheese, mayonnaise, green bell pepper and purple onion. Mix to combine the ingredients. Just before serving, sprinkle the crushed corn chips over the corn. Serve the salad at room temperature or chilled.

Wild Rice and Corn Salad

Makes 4 cups

1 cup cooked wild rice
3 cups cooked whole kernel corn
1/2 cup mayonnaise
3 green onions, chopped
8 oz. can water chestnuts, drained and chopped
1/4 tsp. salt
1/4 tsp. black pepper

Add all the ingredients to a serving bowl. Stir until all the ingredients are combined. Cover the bowl and chill for 2 hours before serving.

Tomato Corn Salad

Makes 6 servings

3 large chopped tomatoes
1/2 cup diced purple onion
1/3 cup green onion
1/4 cup balsamic vinegar
3 tbs. minced fresh basil
1 tbs. minced fresh cilantro
1 tsp. salt
1/2 tsp. black pepper
4 cups fresh corn
3 garlic cloves, peeled and thinly sliced
2 tbs. olive oil
1 tbs. Dijon mustard

In a serving bowl, add the tomatoes, purple onion, green onion, balsamic vinegar, basil, cilantro, salt and black pepper. Toss until combined. In a skillet over medium heat, add the corn, garlic and olive oil. Saute the corn for 6 minutes or until the corn is tender. Remove the skillet from the heat and stir in the Dijon mustard. Add the corn to the vegetables in the bowl. Toss until combined and serve.

Corn Soup with Pico de Gallo

Makes 6 servings

6 corn tortillas, 6" size
4 ears fresh corn, husked
1/2 tsp. vegetable oil
3/4 tsp. salt
3/4 tsp. black pepper
1/2 tsp. paprika
1 cup purple onion, chopped
1 bacon slice, chopped
7 garlic cloves, minced
1/4 cup all purpose flour
3 cups chicken broth
1 cup whole milk
4 oz. can chopped green chiles
1 tsp. ground cumin
1 tsp. dried oregano
1/2 cup minced fresh cilantro
1/4 cup lime juice
2 plum tomatoes, chopped
1 avocado, peeled and chopped
1 serrano pepper, seeded and chopped

Cut the corn tortillas into thin strips. Spray a baking sheet with non stick cooking spray. Place the tortilla strips, in a single layer, on the baking sheet. Preheat the oven to 350°. Bake the strips for 10 minutes or until they are crispy. Remove the strips from the oven and set aside for now. Leave the oven on.

Rub the ears of corn with vegetable oil. Sprinkle 1/2 teaspoon salt, 1/2 teaspoon black pepper and paprika over the corn. Place the corn on a baking sheet. Cook for 20 minutes or until the corn is lightly browned. Turn the corn two times while baking so all sides are evenly browned. Remove the corn from the oven and cool for 15 minutes.

Corn Soup with Pico de Gallo cont'd

Remove the corn from the cob and place in a mixing bowl. In a dutch oven over medium heat, add the onion and bacon. Cook for 5 minutes or until the onion is tender and the bacon crispy. Add 6 garlic cloves to the pan and cook for 1 minute. Sprinkle the all purpose flour over the onion, garlic and bacon. Stir until well combined and cook for 1 minute. Add the chicken broth to the pan. Stir constantly and cook for 2 minutes or until the soup thickens and bubbles.

Add the corn, milk, green chiles, cumin and oregano to the pan. Stir until well combined and the soup is thoroughly heated. Do not let the soup boil once you add the milk. Remove the pan from the heat.

While the soup is cooking, make the pico de gallo. In a serving bowl, add the cilantro, lime juice, tomatoes, avocado, serrano pepper, 1 garlic clove, 1/4 teaspoon salt and 1/4 teaspoon black pepper. Toss until combined.

Spoon the soup into bowls. Top each serving with pico de gallo. Sprinkle the tortilla strips over the soup and serve.

Creamy Chicken Corn Soup

Makes 4 servings

4 oz. boneless skinless chicken thighs, 4 oz. each
2 cans cream of chicken soup, 10.75 oz. size
2 1/4 cups chicken broth
1 cup chopped carrots
1 cup finely chopped onion
1 cup frozen whole kernel corn
1/2 cup chopped celery
1/2 cup water
2 bacon slices, cooked and crumbled

Spray a 4 quart slow cooker with non stick cooking spray. Place the chicken thighs in the slow cooker. In a mixing bowl, add the cream of chicken soup, chicken broth, carrots, onion, corn, celery and water. Stir until combined and pour over the chicken thighs.

Set the temperature to low and cook for 6 hours or until the chicken thighs are tender. Remove the chicken thighs from the slow cooker. Shred the chicken or cut the chicken into cubes. Add the chicken back to the slow cooker. Add the bacon to the slow cooker. Stir until combined and serve.

Shitake, Shrimp and Corn Soup

Makes 8 cups

8 oz. fresh shrimp, peeled and deveined
1 leek, minced
1/2 cup chopped onion
1/4 cup olive oil
2 garlic cloves, minced
3 cups fresh corn kernels
3 cups chicken broth
16 shitake mushrooms, stems removed
1/4 tsp. salt
1/4 tsp. black pepper

In a dutch oven over medium heat, add the leek, onion and 2 tablespoons olive oil. Saute the leek and onion for 2 minutes. Add the garlic and saute the garlic for 2 minutes. Add the corn and 2 1/4 cups chicken broth to the pan. Stir until all the ingredients are combined. Bring the soup to a boil and reduce the heat to low. Simmer for 40 minutes. Remove the pan from the heat. Cool the soup for 10 minutes.

In a skillet over medium heat, add 2 tablespoons olive oil and the mushrooms. Saute the mushrooms for 5 minutes or until they are tender. Sprinkle the salt and black pepper over the mushrooms. Remove the skillet from the heat.

Add the corn mixture to a food processor. Process until smooth and combined. Pour the puree back into the pan. Add 3/4 cup chicken broth to the pan. Place the pan back on the stove over medium heat. Add the mushrooms and shrimp to the pan. Cook for 4 minutes or until the shrimp turn pink. Remove the pan from the heat and serve.

Bacon Corn Soup

Makes 4 servings

2 cups fresh corn kernels
1 cup water
2 cups whole milk
1 tsp. granulated sugar
1 tsp. salt
1/4 tsp. black pepper
2 tbs. unsalted butter
6 slices bacon, cooked and crumbled
1/4 cup minced fresh parsley
1/4 cup minced green onions

In a heavy sauce pan over medium heat, add the corn and water. Bring the corn to a boil. Reduce the heat to medium low and simmer the corn for 10 minutes or until the corn is tender. Stir frequently to keep the corn from sticking and burning.

Add the milk, granulated sugar, salt, black pepper and butter. Stir constantly and cook for 3 minutes. Do not let the soup boil once you add the milk. The soup only needs to be heated. Stir in the bacon. Remove the soup from the heat and ladle into bowls. Top each bowl with parsley and green onions.

Southern Corn Camp Stew

Makes 6 servings

2 1/2 cups frozen whole kernel corn, thawed
1 cup chicken broth
2 tbs. white vinegar
1 tbs. light brown sugar
1/4 cup tomato paste
14 oz. can diced tomatoes
1 1/2 cups cooked lima beans
1/4 cup diced red bell pepper
3 1/2 cups shredded cooked chicken

In a dutch oven over medium heat, add the corn, chicken broth, white vinegar, brown sugar, tomato paste, tomatoes with juice, lima beans and red bell pepper. Stir until all the ingredients are combined.

Bring the soup to a boil and reduce the heat to low. Place a lid on the pan and simmer the soup for 10 minutes or until the corn is tender. Stir in the chicken and cook only until the chicken is thoroughly heated. Remove the pan from the heat and serve.

Corn & Bean Vegetable Soup

Makes 5 servings

1 1/4 cups chicken broth
2 carrots, diced
2 celery ribs, diced
1/2 cup potato, peeled and diced
1/2 cup chopped onion
1 1/2 cups fresh or frozen whole kernel corn
2 cups cooked great northern beans
1 cup whole milk
1 tsp. dried thyme
1/4 tsp. garlic powder
Black pepper to taste

In a large sauce pan over medium heat, add the chicken broth, carrots, celery, potato and onion. Bring the vegetables to a boil and cook for 10 minutes or until the vegetables are tender.

Add the corn, great northern beans, milk, thyme and garlic powder to the pan. Stir until combined and cook for 5 minutes or until the corn is tender. Remove the pan from the heat and season to taste with black pepper.

Corn & Squash Soup

Makes 8 servings

12 bacon slices, diced
1 cup chopped onion
1 celery rib, chopped
2 tbs. all purpose flour
1 3/4 cups chicken broth
6 cups mashed and cooked butternut squash
2 cups cream style corn
2 cups half and half
1 tbs. minced fresh parsley
1 1/2 tsp. salt
1/2 tsp. black pepper
1/2 cup sour cream

In a large sauce pan over medium heat, add the bacon. Cook about 6 minutes or until the bacon is crispy. Remove the bacon from the pan and drain on paper towels. Leave the bacon drippings in the pan. Add the onion and celery to the pan. Saute the vegetables for 5 minutes or until they are tender. Sprinkle the all purpose flour over the vegetables. Stir constantly and cook for 2 minutes.

Add the chicken broth to the pan. Stir constantly and cook until the soup thickens and bubbles. Add the squash, corn, half and half, parsley, salt and black pepper to the pan. Stir constantly and cook only until the soup is thoroughly heated. Do not let the soup boil. Stir in the cooked bacon and remove the pan from the heat.

Spoon the soup into bowls and place a dollop of sour cream over each serving.

Southwest Potato Corn Chowder

Makes 5 servings

6 red potatoes, cut into 1/2" cubes
3 cups chicken broth
1 1/4 tsp. granulated sugar
1/2 tsp. garlic salt
1/4 tsp. black pepper
1/4 tsp. cayenne pepper
1 1/2 cups frozen whole kernel corn, thawed
1/3 cup roasted red bell pepper, chopped
1/3 cup all purpose flour
1 cup whole milk
1 cup shredded sharp cheddar cheese
3/4 cup plain yogurt
1/4 cup finely chopped green onion
3 tbs. chopped fresh cilantro

In a large sauce pan over medium heat, add the potatoes. Cover the potatoes with water and bring the potatoes to a boil. When the potatoes are boiling, reduce the heat to low. Place a lid on the pan and simmer the potatoes for 12 minutes or until the potatoes are tender. Remove the pan from the heat and drain all the water from the potatoes.

In a small bowl, add 1 cup potatoes. Using a fork, mash the potatoes. Add the mashed potatoes, remaining potatoes, chicken broth, granulated sugar, garlic salt, black pepper, cayenne pepper, corn, red bell pepper, all purpose flour and milk to the pan. Place the pan back on the stove over medium heat. Stir constantly and cook until the chowder thickens and bubbles.

Remove the pan from the heat. Stir in the cheddar cheese and yogurt. Stir until the cheese melts. Stir in the green onion and cilantro right before serving.

Sausage Corn Chili

Makes 6 servings

1 lb. ground Italian sausage
1 tbs. dried minced onion
16 oz. can red kidney beans, rinsed and drained
2 cups cooked whole kernel corn
15 oz. can tomato sauce
2/3 cup picante sauce
1/2 cup water
1 tsp. chili powder

In a large sauce pan over medium heat, add the sausage and onion. Stir frequently to break the sausage into crumbles as it cooks. Cook for 10 minutes or until the sausage is well browned and no longer pink. Drain off any excess grease from the sausage.

Add the kidney beans, corn, tomato sauce, picante sauce, water and chili powder to the pan. Stir constantly and bring the chili to a boil. Once the chili is boiling, reduce the heat to low. Simmer for 10 minutes. Remove the chili from the heat and serve.

Cajun Corn Chowder

Makes 2 quarts

1 cup chopped onion
1 green bell pepper, chopped
2 tbs. unsalted butter
1 3/4 cups chicken broth
2 1/2 cups cubed red potatoes
1 jalapeno pepper, chopped
2 tsp. Dijon mustard
1 tsp. salt
1/2 tsp. paprika
1/2 tsp. crushed red pepper flakes
3 cups frozen whole kernel corn, thawed
4 green onions, chopped
3 cups whole milk
1/4 cup all purpose flour

In a dutch oven over medium heat, add the onion, green bell pepper and butter. Saute the vegetables for 5 minutes. Add the chicken broth and potatoes to the pan. Bring the potatoes to a boil and cook for 10 minutes or until the potatoes are tender.

Add the jalapeno pepper, Dijon mustard, salt, paprika, red pepper flakes and corn. Stir until combined and bring the corn to a boil. When the corn is boiling, add the green onions and 2 1/2 cups milk. Stir until well combined.

In a small bowl, add 1/2 cup milk and all purpose flour. Stir until combined and add to the chowder. Stir constantly and cook for 3 minutes or until the chowder thickens and bubbles. Remove the chowder from the heat and serve.

Mexican Chicken Corn Chowder

Makes 6 servings

4 boneless skinless chicken breast, 6 oz. each
1/2 cup chopped onion
2 garlic cloves, minced
3 tbs. unsalted butter
1 cup hot water
2 tsp. instant chicken bouillon granules
1 tsp. ground cumin
2 cups half and half
2 cups shredded Monterey Jack cheese
2 cups cream style corn
4 oz. can diced green chiles
1/4 tsp. Tabasco sauce
1 cup diced tomato

Cut the chicken breast into bite size pieces. In a dutch oven over medium heat, add the chicken, onion, garlic and butter. Saute the chicken for 6 minutes or until the chicken is no longer pink. Add the hot water, chicken bouillon granules and cumin. Stir until well combined and bring the chowder to a boil. When the chowder is boiling, reduce the heat to low.

Place a lid on the pan and simmer the chowder for 5 minutes. Stir in the half and half, Monterey Jack cheese, corn, green chiles with liquid and Tabasco sauce. Stir constantly and cook only until the cheese melts and the chowder is thoroughly heated. Do not let the chowder come to a boil once you add the half and half. Remove the chowder from the heat and stir in the tomato. Serve hot.

CHAPTER INDEX

Appetizers & Dips

Hot Corn Dip, 2
Field Pea & Corn Dip, 3
Mexicorn Salsa, 3
Corn and Avocado Salsa, 4
Grilled Corn Salsa, 5
Roasted Corn & Avocado Dip, 6
Chorizo Corn Relish, 7
Corn Relish, 8
Sweet Corn and Tomato Relish, 9

Main Dishes & Casseroles

Beefy Corn Nachos, 11
Hamburger Corn Casserole, 12
Corn Stuffed Butterfly Pork Chops, 13
Baked Black Bean & Corn Salsa Pork Chops, 14
Grilled Mexican Pork Chops, 15
Smoky Corn & Chicken Salad, 16
Sauteed Spicy Sausage & Corn Salad, 17
Andouille & Corn Skillet, 18
Simple Chicken Corn Wraps, 18
Grilled Corn & Squash Quesadillas, 19
Cheesy Corn Pie, 20
Corn and Squash Frittata, 21
Country Corn Omelet, 22

Breads

Cheddar Cornbread, 24
Crawfish Cornbread, 25
Creole Cornbread, 26
Whole Kernel Corn Cornbread, 27
Cheesy Italian Corn Squares, 28
Cheddar Lemon Corn Muffins, 29
Corn Waffles with Cilantro Lime Butter, 30
Roasted Corn and Lobster Beignets, 31
Corn and Crab Fritters, 33

Soups, Salads & Sides

Corn and Asiago Bread Pudding, 35
Parmesan Corn Pudding, 36
Southern Corn Pudding, 37
Green Chile Corn Pudding, 38
Corn Chive Flan, 39
Fiesta Corn Rice Casserole, 40
Green Bean & Corn Casserole, 41
Creamy Corn & Broccoli Side Dish, 42
Tex Mex Rice & Corn, 43
Company Corn, 44
Cayenne Corn, 45
Southern Cream Corn, 46
Corn & Zucchini Skillet, 47
Roasted Corn & Garlic Chipotle Mashed Potatoes, 48
Swiss Corn Bake, 49
Creamy Sweet Corn, 50
Southern Fried Corn, 50
Buttermilk Fried Corn, 51
Spicy Baked Pepper Corn, 52
Cheesy Corn Bake, 53
Corn Stuffed Zucchini, 54
Ancho Chili Corn, 55
Grilled Southwestern Corn, 56
Chili Lime Grilled Corn, 57
Baked Indian Corn, 58
Cream Cheese Baked Corn on the Cob, 59
Grilled Corn with Red Chile Paste, 60
Grilled Corn with Jalapeno Lime Butter, 61
Grilled Garlic Chive Corn on the Cob, 62
Grilled Corn with Maple Vinaigrette, 63
Creole Grilled Corn, 64
Grilled Corn with Creamy Chipotle Sauce, 65
Smoked Thyme Butter Corn, 66
Grilled Sweet Corn & Peppers, 67
Garlic Pepper Corn, 68
Bacon and Caramelized Onion Corn, 69
Grilled Chili Bacon Corn, 70
Field Peas, Corn & Okra, 71
Barbecued Corn, 72

Soups, Salads & Sides cont'd

Sunshine Casserole, 72
Scalloped Corn and Potatoes, 73
Fresh Corn Vinaigrette, 74
Barley Corn Salad, 75
Marinated Zucchini Corn Salad, 76
Grilled Avocado Corn Poblano Salad, 77
Grilled Italian Corn Salad, 78
Roasted Corn and Black Bean Salad, 79
Fresh Corn Salad, 80
Taco Corn Salad, 81
Creamy Corn Salad, 81
Crunchy Corn Salad, 82
Wild Rice and Corn Salad, 82
Tomato Corn Salad, 83
Corn Soup with Pico de Gallo, 84
Creamy Chicken Corn Soup, 86
Shitake, Shrimp and Corn Soup, 87
Bacon Corn Soup, 88
Southern Corn Camp Stew, 89
Corn & Bean Vegetable Soup, 90
Corn & Squash Soup, 91
Southwest Potato Corn Chowder, 92
Sausage Corn Chili, 93
Cajun Corn Chowder, 94
Mexican Chicken Corn Chowder, 95

ABOUT THE AUTHOR

Lifelong southerner who lives in Bowling Green, KY. Priorities in life are God, family and pets. I love to cook, garden and feed most any stray animal that walks into my yard. I love old cookbooks and cookie jars. Huge NBA fan who loves to spend hours watching basketball games. Enjoy cooking for family and friends and hosting parties and reunions. Can't wait each year to build gingerbread houses for the kids.

Printed in Great
Britain
by Amazon